Sp⊙t the Differences

Differences

Picture Puzzles for Kids

PHOTO ALTERING BY
PETER DONAHUE

DOVER PUBLICATIONS, INC.
MINEOLA, NEW YORK

Bibliographical Note

Spot the Differences Picture Puzzles for Kids is a new work, first published
by Dover Publications, Inc., in 2014.

International Standard Book Number

ISBN-13: 978-0-486-78248-5
ISBN-10: 0-486-78248-4

Manufactured in the United States by LSC Communications
78248406   2019
www.doverpublications.com

Inside this book you'll find twenty-five spot-the-differences challenges. Each puzzle contains two brightly colored photographs—the page on the left contains the original picture, while the page on the right adds 10 to 14 changes for you to find. Try your best to complete each puzzle on your own—check boxes are provided to help you track your progress—but if you get stuck, just turn to the Answers section, which begins on page 54.

TURN BOOK!

☐ ☐ ☐ ☐ ☐ ☐ ☐ ☐ ☐ ☐ ☐ ☐ ☐

Keep Score: 13 Changes

Keep Score: 11 Changes ☐ ☐ ☐ ☐ ☐ ☐ ☐ ☐ ☐ ☐ ☐

Keep Score: 11 Changes   □ □ □ □ □ □ □ □ □ □ □

TURN BOOK!

Keep Score: **10** Changes ☐ ☐ ☐ ☐ ☐ ☐ ☐ ☐ ☐ ☐

KEEP SCORE: 11 CHANGES □ □ □ □ □ □ □ □ □ □ □

Keep Score: 11 Changes ☐ ☐ ☐ ☐ ☐ ☐ ☐ ☐ ☐ ☐ ☐

KEEP SCORE: 11 Changes ☐ ☐ ☐ ☐ ☐ ☐ ☐ ☐ ☐ ☐ ☐

Pages 4 - 5

1. Handprint added
2. Smiley face removed
3. Hair clip added
4. Black line on wall removed
5. Cartoon hand on wall added
6. Paintbrush in hand added
7. Design on pink pants added
8. Yinyang symbol added
9. Blue bottle added
10. Paintbrush removed

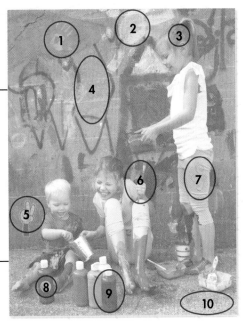

istockphoto ©Lilja Kristjansdottir

Pages 6 - 7

1. Spider added
2. Yellow candy added
3. Sign text removed
4. Big lollipop added
5. White egg candy added
6. Green heart candy added
7. Pink candy added
8. Cookies added
9. Green gummy bears added
10. Purple gummy bear added

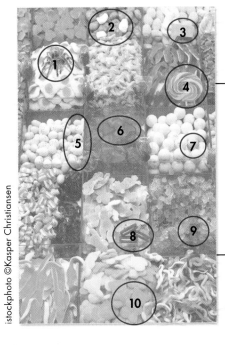

istockphoto ©Kasper Christiansen

Pages 8 - 9

1. Foam hand added
2. Beard added
3. Green pom-pom
4. Purple foam hand
5. Glasses added
6. Arrow on sign added
7. Hair covering ear
8. Text on foam hand removed
9. "9" hole removed
10. "1" on blue shirt added

©Fuse

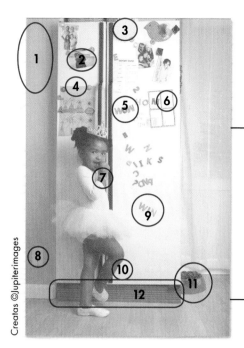

Pages 10 - 11

1. Phone removed
2. Dog photo
3. Sun face removed
4. Blue "T" removed
5. "MOM" changed to "WOW"
6. "E" removed
7. Bracelet added
8. Outlet added
9. "WIN" added
10. Star wand removed
11. Dog food bowl added
12. Grey refrigerator base

Creatas ©Jupiterimages

Pages 12 - 13

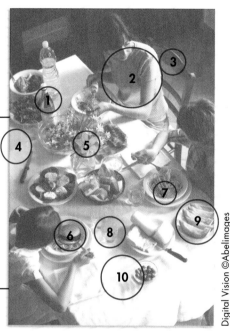

1. Label on bottle removed
2. Pink shirt
3. Chair hole removed
4. Missing spaghetti bowl
5. Purple flower added
6. Hamburger added
7. Meatball added
8. Water glass added
9. Extra cantaloupe slices added
10. Knife removed

Digital Vision ©Abelimages

Pages 14 - 15

1. Extra plates added
2. Blue cup
3. "HERB" added
4. Flower pot added
5. Yellow cup
6. Design on blue vase added
7. Rubber duckie added
8. Branch with berries shortened
9. Grey fence changed to brown
10. Red cup
11. Ball of yarn added

istockphoto ©belchonock

Pages 16-17

1. Boy removed
2. Net handle shortened
3. Shell on bathing suit added
4. Flower on hat added
5. Airplane added
6. Orange stripe on hat
7. Black pattern on bathing suit removed
8. Shell added
9. Boat added
10. Moon added
11. Green sunglasses
12. Octopus on tube added
13. Red dots on bathing suit removed

istockphoto ©YanLev

Pages 18-19

1. Scale removed
2. "WOOF" sign added
3. Poster changed
4. Green monkey toy removed
5. Wristwatch removed
6. Blue stripe on dog pillow
7. Extra dog leg
8. Dog hair color changed
9. Purple dog harness
10. Water bowl added

©Fuse

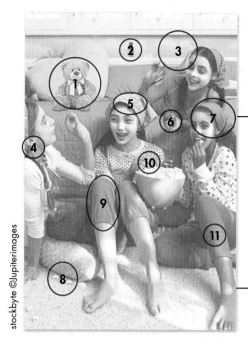

Pages 20-21

1. Teddy bear added
2. Nail polish bottle added
3. Foot removed
4. Earring added
5. Green bandana pattern changed
6. Apple added
7. Orange bandana
8. Extra popcorn on floor
9. Blue sweatpant leg
10. Color of nail polish changed
11. Ladybug design on pants added

stockbyte ©Jupiterimages

Pages 22-23

1. Window missing
2. Green door
3. Hamburger added
4. Zoo poster added
5. Flower pot added
6. Barred-window removed
7. U.S.A. flag flopped
8. Long window added
9. Demon grafitti added
10. Windows shortened
11. Hinges removed
12. Door added
13. Small windows added
14. Aquarium background added

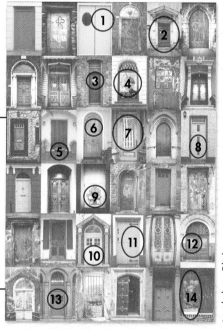

istockphoto ©littleny

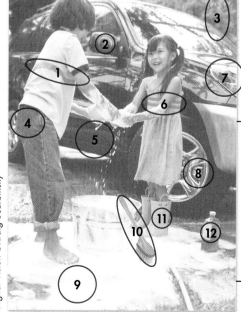

Digital Vision ©Kraig Scarbinsky

Pages 24-25

1. Pink stripe on shirt added
2. Peace symbol on car mirror added
3. Tree trunk removed
4. Back pocket removed
5. Soap drops removed
6. Dark green stripes on dress added
7. Green headlight
8. Car hubcap changed
9. Hose removed
10. Brush added
11. Flower on boot removed
12. Amount of soap in bottle reduced

Pages 26 - 27

1. Balloon moved to the left
2. Clouds added
3. Plane added
4. Balloon removed
5. Balloon added
6. Red patch on large balloon
7. Balloon removed
8. Green patch on balloon on ground
9. "Happy Birthday" balloon added
10. "Peace" design on truck added
11. Woman added
12. Elephant added

Hemera ©Iryna Kurhan

Pages 28 - 29

1. White bars removed
2. Long bar added
3. Shoulder strap removed
4. Yellow belt on denim dress added
5. Blue bracelets
6. Blue shirt
7. Strap hanging down added
8. Green dress in mirror
9. Heart pattern on dress changed
10. Dog added
11. Sneaker added

Digital Vision ©Digital Vision

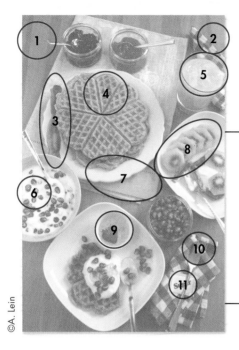

Pages 30 - 31

1. Spoon handle shortened
2. Corner of napkin removed
3. Bacon added
4. Waffle slice added
5. Ice in orange juice added
6. Blueberries added
7. Blue napkin corner
8. Kiwi slices added
9. Strawberry added
10. Fork tine removed
11. Sugar packet added

©A. Lein

Pages 32 - 33

1. Branch in window added
2. Fingers removed
3. Black accordion key removed
4. Dark pink shirt
5. Rip in jeans added
6. Band-aid added
7. Yellow books
8. Orange skirt
9. Pencil cup added
10. Papers removed
11. Chair leg removed

stockbyte ©Jupiterimages

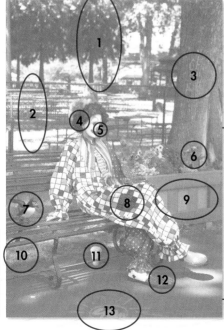

Pages 34 - 35

1. Tree removed
2. Fence pole removed
3. Initials carved in tree added
4. Purple hair
5. Green nose
6. Pink flower added
7. Bird added
8. Red squares on pants added
9. Color of wooden boards changed
10. Bench leg removed
11. Coffe cup added
12. Stars on shoe removed
13. Chalk sun added

Photodisc ©Jen Siska

Pages 36-37

1. "Happy" color changed
2. Orange slice added
3. Red jelly bean removed
4. Cracked glass
5. Green candy added
6. Blue fruit slice gummy
7. Red candy added
8. Purple candy added
9. Swirls added to green candy
10. Yellow candy removed

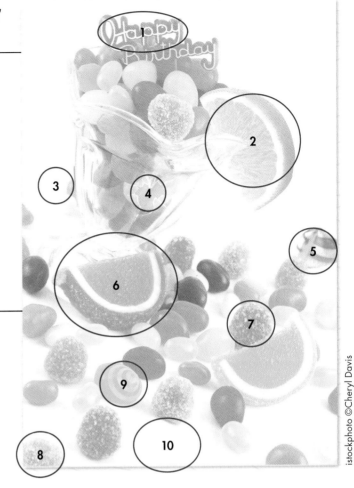

istockphoto ©Cheryl Davis

Pages 38-39

1. Green party hat
2. "B" removed
3. Happy face added
4. T-shirt design added
5. Earring added
6. Glasses added
7. "Happy" removed
8. Gold party hat removed
9. Amount of juice in pitcher changed
10. Soda color changed

istockphoto ©Shironosov

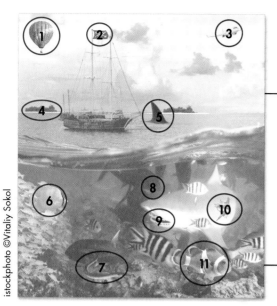

istockphoto ©Vitaliy Sokol

Pages 40 - 41

1. Hot air balloon added
2. Pirate flag added
3. Airplane added
4. Island added
5. Shark fin added
6. Butterfly fish added
7. Eel added
8. Tiny fish removed
9. Silly teeth added
10. Tattoo added
11. Clown fish added

Pages 42 - 43

1. Chimney added
2. Chimney removed
3. Window removed
4. Window flowers added
5. Flag added
6. Blue shutters
7. "Café" sign added
8. Shutters style changed
9. Fire hydrant added
10. Garbage can added
11. Shutters style changed

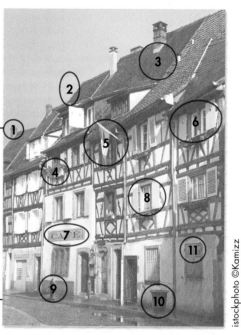

istockphoto ©Kamizz

stockbyte ©Jupiterimages

Pages 44 - 45

1. Sign added
2. Leafy branch added
3. Eyebrow removed
4. Sunglasses added
5. Lollipop added
6. Green shirt
7. Belt added
8. Pink glove
9. Necklace added
10. Rose added
11. Spout removed

Pages 46-47

1. Bar on shelf removed
2. White containers removed
3. Small orange container removed
4. Orange liquid
5. Bolt on door removed
6. "Fruit Punch" label added
7. Silly glasses added
8. Yinyang magnet added
9. Pickle jar added
10. T-shirt artwork added
11. Bookmark added
12. Amount of green liquid changed

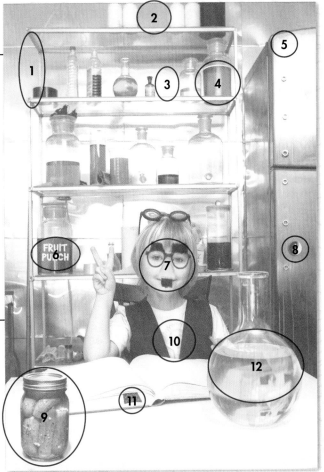

istockphoto ©Viktor Kamynin

Pages 48-49

1. Ring removed
2. White square ring changed
3. Sun added to blue ring
4. Green ring changed to pink
5. Red beads removed
6. Ring with red circle added
7. Green ring
8. Pink ovals added
9. Bracelets removed
10. Gold ring changed to blue

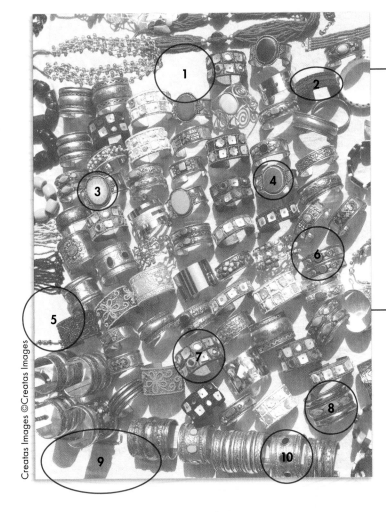

Creatas Images ©Creatas Images

Pages 50 - 51

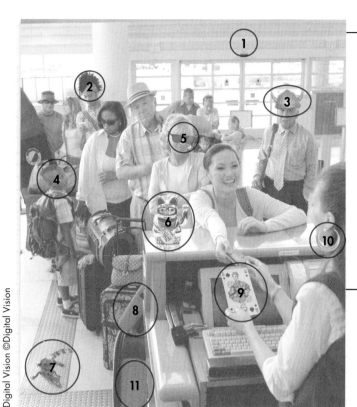

1. Exit sign removed
2. Mohawk hairstyle added
3. Viking hat added
4. Boy's head turned
5. Sunglasses added
6. Good-luck cat statue added
7. Baby alligator added
8. Green bag
9. Paper changed
10. Earring added
11. Suitcase handle removed

Digital Vision ©Digital Vision

Pages 52 - 53

1. Striped hat extended
2. Mini-hat removed
3. Sunglasses added
4. Stripe on hat added
5. Microphone added
6. Blue star removed
7. Rope on drum removed
8. Pink star on dress
9. Stripe on shorts removed
10. Rainbow sock added

Blend Images ©Ariel Skelley